SHENESIA EWING

UNCOVERING the NEW U

"CHANGE YOUR MIND, CHANGE YOUR CIRCUMSTANCES!"

Copyright © 2018 by SheNesia Ewing

All rights reserved. No part of this publication may be reproduced, distributed, or transmitted in any form or by any means, including photocopying, recording, or other electronic or mechanical methods, without the prior written permission of the Publisher, except in the case of brief quotations embodied in critical reviews and certain other noncommercial uses permitted by copyright law. For permission requests, write to the author, addressed "Attention: Permissions Coordinator," at the address below.

SheNesia Ewing
authornesiewing@gmail.com
www.AuthorNesiEwing.com

Copyright © 2018 SheNesia Ewing

All rights reserved.

ISBN: 978-0-692-13662-1

THIS BOOK IS DEDICATED TO:

My Son, Husband, Mother, Father, and Big Brother

Table of Contents

Acknowledgement vii

Introduction ix

1. The Bricks They Threw 1
2. The Blessing 19
3. Processes to Success 33
4. All U Need is '1' Chance 43
5. Change Your Mind Change Your Circumstance 53
6. Building and Rebuilding Bridges 61
7. The Spine 69
8. Nothing Stands Between U and Success But U 85
9. Set Back or Set Up? 93
10. Change Begins With U 99

LET'S WERK 102

About The Author 107

Acknowledgement

I would first like to give honor to God for providing me with the required strength to scale through the struggles I came across over the years. It is because of my faith that has pushed me along as far as I have come.

I would also like to thank my mother Delores Hopkins for believing in me and always pushing me to go further than the hurdles that stood before me. U supported me, encouraged me, and laughed with me. U even cried with me during the times I didn't know whether to give up or keep going. Despite sacrifices made, U stuck with me and I thank U for that, I appreciate U, and I love U.

Furthermore, I would like to thank my father, Willie Hopkins III, for teaching me to be headstrong. U taught me the true meaning of the saying, **"God didn't build us to break, He built us to build"**! Forcing me to work hard for whatever I desired in life. Thank U, Daddy!

Above all, I would like to thank my Husband, Fred Ewing. My love, U have given me more than I deserve. I appreciate your love, sacrifice, care, and willingness to not just get me through but make it through with me. I appreciate the support through the long nights and the encouragement to keep going and not quit in this process. U believed in me, and I can't thank U enough for choosing me to be your life.

To my brother Will, man U are the best brother a sister could have. We have been through somethings and I need U to know that I appreciate every moment we've shared good and bad. It is because of your constant belief in me that I can do anything, that I am going after just that. I made a promise and I am keeping it. See U at the top. I love U!

To my son, Xavier; U have also given me the courage I needed to get where I am today. One day, I hope U will understand the purpose of all my sacrifices. They were made to help U understand that the sky is not just the limit, but a new starting point for higher greatness in life. I love U with all my heart never forget that!

Introduction

To my S.H.E readers (Strong, Healthy, & Empowered), I thank U for purchasing my first self-published book. I pray that U will be motivated to trust in yourself and your abilities to know that anything is possible. There is nothing in this world that can't be accomplished by U if U continually push through the circumstances. U can begin by changing your perspective to see your oppositions as OPPORTUNITIES.

Every day U work towards your goals and dreams brings U closer to birthing your purpose and living for that purpose intentionally. Trust yourself and remember that every challenge is simply a test of your efforts and the strength already domicile in U. So, USE IT! Use it to your advantage because it's YOURS. Nothing in the world will come to U if U don't believe in who U are, what U stand for, and what U desire to achieve.

I hope that U find this book an eye opener that just because your success was delayed that it isn't denied. Nothing can deny U but U. It is in those challenging moments where if I could turn back the hands of time I would not, because I would not be where I am today, and I can now teach others how to avoid getting there.

Nothing in life comes easy but it is what we work so hard for that we seek reward and gratification. Remember to Uncover the new U, change begins with U; but for change to begin, U must change your mind to change those circumstances.

Challenges make you discover things about yourself that you never really knew.

~ Cicely Tyson

1

The Bricks They Threw

I would not have thought that my life would be where it is right now. When I was 13 years of age, I used to tell myself that I was going to law school. And not just any law school, but one of the top law schools in the country. And also to find an amazing husband who would give me all that I could ever want, these which include the desire to have 13 children. As far-fetched as it may have sounded, I only have one biological brother, one living god brother, and sister, and one deceased. I think just like most of us, I desired the American Dream; large family, white picket fenced home, and a progressive career. Did U once have the same vision in your life or something different than where U are now? I can only begin to imagine where U wanted to be and just how different things are right now.

Whenever I begin to look back over my life, I am always very confident that I am right where I am supposed to be. As a woman, I know that I was put here, right now, in this place for a reason. The highs and lows of life forced me to fight for the spot that I have in life currently. I've experienced rape, alcoholism, homelessness, repossessions, abusive relationships, neglect, being talked about, brokenness, depression, and so much more. Knowing how I grew up, I had the strength inside to do whatever I had to do to be the best version of myself every day. I knew I could be the mother I was designed to be, and the wife I was cultivated to be. And I was positive it would happen one day.

My social support system wavered most of my life. I found it true that when people show U who they are, BELIEVE THEM. I had more people against me than for me, and it was discouraging. I had to understand that it was me all along who needed to believe in me! How often have U told someone that U didn't need their stamp of approval on something, knowing deep down U wanted it? I happened to have said it repeatedly and even backed it up with the expression of confidence on my face, but inside, it never existed until now. It wasn't until I understood me, that I noticed the people in my circle where only there just because of me. Despite the storm, I didn't give up, I didn't fail, and my faith didn't waiver. My experience was my testimony, and my oppositions became my opportunities.

I don't know about U, but I am always annoyed with the common saying that some things are better left alone than said and my mother raised me this way to some extent. Because of this I never fully comprehended how to work my way through issues, extreme emotional and self-inflicted pain. It took me to a place where I became afraid of having too MANY emotions or not having enough, and became angry at the drop of a dime. Sometimes, looking from the outside in, one would classify me as unstable, and that wasn't healthy. But being delivered from myself had to be one of the hardest and the biggest challenges to date that I've had to face.

Going back all the way to elementary school, I didn't know what the real-life people often spoke of. The only job given to me by my parents was to go to school and focus on getting through normal childhood challenges. Do U still remember those days? No responsibility, no real hardships, just growing up and learning to prepare for what life had in store for U. Those were the days of no concern at all. Sometimes, I would wish I could return, especially not having any bills to pay LOL.

The events that took place in high school were the catalyst of how I ended up where I am today. In high-school, U would think those would be the memories that U would want to hold on to and never forget. But for me, I do not desire to keep most of those memories. Remembering times of being bullied, tormented, and raped, lead me to develop serious self-esteem issues. Memories such as these would force some to contemplate if anyone would even care if they were gone. I would assume that no one likes rejection, or do U like it? The constant rejection I experienced pushed me into solitude. My thoughts were dark, and I hid behind a mask that slowly began to fall off the closer I got to high school graduation. High school was supposed to give U new friends and experiences, and also provide a gateway to uncover who U truly are. Why didn't that happen for me? Why was I singled out? Despite my loneliness and desire to belong by the end of graduation, I was left with an unborn secret only questioning my existence.

"Solitude is no place for sorrows"
~ Life Coach Nesi

At the age of 16, I was in love with someone I didn't know existed and someone I would never get a chance to know. I found myself dealing with an older man who took from me something I could never get back; my innocence, my virginity. For four months, I watched my belly grow never knowing what or how I was going to take care of what was inside. I was ashamed of what happened because this is not how I ever expected my first time to be. The kissing, the holding, the flowers, with someone U love, the sweet talk; the intimacy, yeah none of that was there.

Mothers are wonderful. They know their children well, and even when something is wrong or the children are up to something, they easily know. My mother knew something was up when I called to ask for a double whopper with cheese no onions or tomatoes supersized with a Dr. Pepper twice in one day. My mother had never heard me ask for such food and that was when she knew something was wrong. When I sat down and told her my story, she touched my belly and cried. She didn't understand how that could have happened to me. The pain in her eyes pierced my soul, and all I knew was that she was disappointed in me, but on the contrary, she wasn't. But because of the stress, I went through, coupled with the lack of necessary care, I lost the baby after some weeks. I was sitting over a toilet, staring down and watching my world fall out of me. There were no words that I could give to explain how I felt. My mothers' words resonated in my ears, "Baby maybe it just wasn't your time"....

I joined the United States Army National Guard in 2001 only because I got tired of asking my parents for money and I didn't want them to pay for my school. Like most parents, my parents were wondering how they were going to pay for my school, what scholarships I was going to apply for, and where I was going to go. Nope, I made the decision that I am going to let the military do it for me, and I must say that was the best decision I ever made. I was active in sports all throughout my high school education and knew that although not active duty being a reservist would bring in additional funds to whatever I was earning from Pizza Inn at the time. When I told my parents that I was going into the Army, I had never seen such happiness in their eyes. They were proud of me for making my first real grown-up decision. Can U remember that feeling?

Go! Go! Go! Grab your stinking bags and hurry up! U've got one minute! Hurry up creeps! Wow, what a culture shock! I had to ask myself what did I just GET myself into as I stepped off the bus at Fort Jackson, SC for basic training. I think I dropped in the front leaning position eight, maybe nine times before the thirty seconds were up. What a traumatic experience, LOL. However, I was so proud of myself. If anyone can survive nine weeks of unknown individuals yelling at them, sleeping outside, getting attacked by fire ants and chiggers, with a PT score of 296 out of 300, they have all the right to be filled with glory. I was a bad lady back then LOL. And I was so excited. By the time I returned home, I had grown so much mentally and physically; but still, I was drowning emotionally.

I wasn't as strong as I thought I was because the desire for acceptance was still there. I wanted that friend who I could call on for anything and would stick by me through thick and thin. All I needed was one. My mother was my confidant but at the end of the day she is not my friend but my mother, and I respected the ramifications of our relationship. Sometimes, some things I wanted to talk about and share were not for my mothers' ears. Shortly after I returned home, I moved to Durham NC, which later became the start of my mental breakdown. I had a roommate who milked everything out of me, used me, moved out, and didn't care about my well-being. When I say she didn't care about my well-being, I meant when she left; she didn't bother ensuring I had everything handled financially or whether I could survive on my own. She didn't dare to ask that important question. Despite her reasons, she walked out on responsibilities; she ran and left me empty handed. I had given up opportunities for school, scholarships, and to think I put the majority of my money on the move for her, thinking I was helping a real friend, my best friend. After all, I had done for her, she didn't give a damn about me, and I was angry and lost trust in people, especially women.

It was the summertime, and I was out on a stroll, and as I stopped for gas, a fine man walked up and pumped my gas without even asking. While I was trying to figure out what he wanted we exchanged words and numbers, and everything was great for the first 30 days, after which things changed overnight.

"U do what I tell U to do and speak when spoken to and that means if I call U, U better answer!" "I didn't have the intention not to call U back, I was working." Who gives a F*** about your job, I am your man, and U will do as I tell U to do. Now apologize before I hit U again." "I am sorry, it won't happen again." It's okay baby I am sorry I get angry because U make me feel like I am less of a man when U don't follow my directions. Do what I ask and there will be no problems…"

This scenario above was what I was dealing with and experienced around three to four times a week. Tay was my first true domestic violence relationship. Before this, a younger guy smacked me when I was in the eighth grade and we immediately broke up. So, I didn't understand why I was much stronger to walk away as an adolescent than I was as an adult. Tay led me to drinking to the point where EverClear didn't even give me a buzz. If U know anything about alcohol, compare this to gasoline, lol. How many people do U know are in such situation, or probably it's U that is afraid to leave someone like Tay who pounded on me at least two times a week for gratification? Well, guess what, now U do. I ALLOWED HIM to make me feel like that, and he told me I was worthless. I was only convenient for him and that I couldn't do any better.

Did U notice how I capitalized "I ALLOWED?" Yes, because I did. I stayed, don't ask me why, but I did. I didn't reach out for help or let anyone know what was going on, because I was embarrassed. I stayed because I didn't know my worth. I let this man destroy my self-esteem, friendships, and most of all me. I might as well have been his prostitute because that is how he treated me just without the financial benefits. He forced me to do things I would have never imagined and inside I knew this was not me. I had to remember the longer I ALLOWED it to keep happening, the longer he was going to keep doing it. I had to find the strength to get up and get out. Although it was hard, I learned it was okay to start over. Sometimes, having ties to your past can keep U linked to what tried to destroy U. So, it is your choice of how long U allow YOUR pain to control U.

My mother always says 'treat others the way U want to be treated,' but that didn't last because after that roommate left, I found another. When I left for my annual training in California for two weeks, she took my rent money and also stole items out of my house. I returned to a padded apartment. She was a young girl who I will never forget. At that time, I wanted to give her a piece of my mind. I was often reminded that no matter how bad someone treats U, U should never allow that to change who U are. That is called power over self. No man (male or female) should ever be given a chance to have more power over U than U have over yourself. I couldn't win for losing! With no money and time, I was forced to move into a drug and roach infested apartment. Not only did I have to pay to get my belongings out of the padded apartment, but I had to pay past rent too. My luck was simply not the greatest, my patience was running thin, and depression was in full fledge.

Sometimes a series of bad luck is a set up for a series of successes, and that alone is something we must remember amid transition of 'Uncovering The New U.' Our experiences are what shape us into becoming who we are. They do not define who we are; rather, they shape us for what we WOULD become.

God must have known; again the THOUGHT began to creep into my head that maybe I would just be better off gone. I went from Durham, NC to the dirt, Iraq. I was enrolled in school for three days at North Carolina Central University and was excited. I desired to join the cheerleading squad and enter the pre-law program. I laugh about this idea every time I think of it. I ran into my Commander at the time, and he asked me, Are U ready? And looking at him dumbfounded I said, for what? He stated that my unit was being mobilized to Iraq. What a fearful situation knowing 9/11 just occurred. I cried all the way to the car and of course, called my mommy. My mother said, "baby, U know what U signed up for; let's be a big girl, tie up our boots, head held high, and ship out ready to protect and defend." I didn't want to hear that then, but that was a response to be reckoned with. If I knew how much power that had then, I sure would not have any reason to complain about life now.

My deployment as a cook in the United States Army National Guard was a rough one. I experienced what it felt like to have no running water as we had to; take bottle water baths, wash our clothes by hand, sleep in tents, and no access to my mother. I was lonely. It was 130 degrees every day, sandstorms that coated my clothing and personal items. There were days I cried and confided in people that were no good for me. I am not proud of it, but I fell in lust with a married man. Nothing sexual but he had my mind and attention. I settled for having him there in that space and time; not caring about what he had at home. These were some of the lowest feelings I had ever had. It is not possible to love something or someone that doesn't or will ever belong to U. How does this happen?

This feeling of self-worthlessness reared its ugly head AGAIN because I was satisfied with being second. Being second isn't winning. Getting the scraps are not winning. Despite feeling safe, feeling loved, and desired, the feelings were not real, nor were they permanent. Understanding my worth was a huge transition, realizing I accepted behaviors such as I have exhibited. But what would U expect, coming from what I had recently come through? I look back, and I had to ask myself, what if that was MY husband? I would be pissed and ready to let her have it! His clothes would end up outside in a shopping cart waiting on the curb for him to pick up. It is however impossible to have double standards. So, choose one but make sure it's the same standard U would want in your own home as well.

Thankfully, at a young age, I found out that SETTLING IS NOT AN OPTION! I am worthy, and I deserve real love and affection in addition to all the things I have worked so hard for. I cannot let anyone tell me that I am LESS than valuable either! I don't care what happened in my past; I had to leave it there and move ON. What I want in life was not going to be behind me!

I didn't want to go back to North Carolina anymore upon my return from Iraq because there were too many burdens I desired not to carry back there. I honestly believed if I had gone back there, I would have lost my mind, being in the same space, doing the same thing, in the same struggle. I needed change! There was a lot of decision making and sacrifices which eventually led me to Virginia. I gave up offers to colleges and also got rid of toxic people around me; this, which allowed me to have a true fresh start. And of course, I didn't regret making those decisions. I just knew things were headed in the right direction; going to college with money from deployment, bills paid and didn't want for much being that the military funded my education and I received stipends for successful coursework. I was excited to meet new friends, I became a cheerleader, and I was HAPPY. Have U ever felt so relieved just to start life over? It makes U say Wow! Right? That was exactly how I felt at that moment.

Throughout my freshman and sophomore years, life was so good. I had the life that I wanted. My mother was a stickler for education and even as an adult, she made sure that education was ALWAYS primary in my life over sports and so at a minimum, my GPA was 3.0 or higher. My cheer coach as well didn't accept anything less than greatness from her girls. She provided a family-oriented structure that separated us from other squads. With such a foundation it helped us cope with being away from home and family.

The purpose for attending college was to continue building on what I had found out about myself while on deployment. Despite all that I had been through emotionally, I knew I still had some work to do on myself. Learning to trust again, love again (not a relationship but people in general), and learning to appreciate who I was becoming. College was supposed to restore what I had lost; I thought it would anyway.

In my junior year, I volunteered for a three-month deployment to assist the United States Border Patrol in Sasabe, Arizona. I must also admit that being in the military allowed me to experience situations that made me stepped out of moral character. I found myself being a sex slave practically to a man that I later got to know had the perception that black women were only good for sex and white women as marriage material. And this was in his words. He believed that if U flashed money in a black woman's face, he automatically had the right to do whatever he wanted and when he wanted. And he was a black man! When I didn't want sex with him, he made life hard for me. Being of a senior rank, he had more say over my day than I did. Attempting to avoid this situation to affect my work ethic, I always did as I was told when on duty. Though I didn't want anything from him, but friendship and it turned into being this.

Still unknown to me how I ended there with him, I realized I was involved with people I shouldn't have ordinarily mingled with and also did things I shouldn't have done. Thinking back mentally, I discovered I didn't understand my worth yet again, I was still lost. I cannot and will not blame it on age; because I knew better and I just chose not to acknowledge. However, I was grateful for this time because my teachers virtually worked with me; that kept me enrolled and also as a full-time student.

Is this starting to sound like a broken record yet?

When I returned home, I was excited to be back and to get back to college, life, and work; but God had other plans for me. Have U ever misjudged the kindness of a person? Someone who played the part of a friend, came close to U because they could, and when a simple situation becomes complicated they leave? After these years of seeking understanding of self and people, I thought I had mastered it, but yet again, I was wrong.

I refused to move back on campus upon my return, so I found an apartment off campus that was affordable for my new roommate and I. We were close and I thought the world of her. Because of her personality, I was confident she was going to be a perfect fit for maintaining all that I had gained. Post-deployment and finances were in good standing once again, and things were moving in the right direction. I wanted someone else around and just because it was her that I was willing to give another shot at having a roommate. As the broken record continues, she later did to me what the first and second roommates did. She found out she was pregnant and moved out to return home and once again, I thought I was going to lose my damn mind.

Now, it is safe to assume that when we meet people, we usually start out as friends. We advance with them to learn everything they are willing to share with us; and sometimes, chaos or drama occurs when essential information is left out in the building of such friendship. I met a man who I considered a friend. He and I had much in common, and for me, there was nothing more that I wanted. I enjoyed the long conversations, the walks to class, and random trips to the Burger King not too far from campus; we had something great going on. I had worn the wrong shirt for the pep rally that evening, and he rode with me to switch out. Thinking nothing of it, I left him in the living room while I freshened up. I later came to find him in my room, and again, one thing led to another. My flesh became so weak and vulnerable after long periods of being untouched. I knew it was a mistake I made, and I wanted to forget what happened and carry on. We both agreed right there that there won't be a second time and it was not to be discussed for any reason.

And for my roommate, I emptied my bank account to pay bills and watched her leave without offering me a dime. After three months, I found out that I was pregnant and had nowhere to go. Pregnant and homeless; what great combination right? With no money to take her to court, I was ass out of $3,000. I had to put my things in storage, and for four months of my pregnancy, it was me and my gold neon. I used to shower at the local gym using the excuse that I was rushing for class and just needed to use the ladies room. Always hungry, I had a food stamp card and could only use the local market for food. It got to the point the cashiers knew my name. This was a struggle knowing I had never lived like this before. My parents didn't raise me to ever want for anything and I had to ask myself why me, why now, and why here? What I didn't realize was this was the best thing that could have happened to me.

I received not a single phone call from the other half of my child. And as often as I waddled around on my college campus, I often saw him walk past me to get to class, and not once did he ever ask how my son or I was doing. Did it bother me, hell yes! He was my friend (so I thought), and I allowed myself to be weakened by man. He wasn't interested in me, my mind, or anything I had to offer but it was what I had in between my legs that he wanted. As hopeful as I was, he was only out for one thing, he got it, and he was out. No need to sugar-coat the situation. What a fool I was then, but it eventually became a fool I refused to stay. Being blinded by charm and kindness is such a common theme, coupled with the desire to be wanted and cared for. I cannot begin to explain how often I thought I was desired, and yet, in the end, it made me out to seem desperate as though I didn't deserve better when I knew I did.

I had to question myself 'why me? What was wrong with me? And why does it seem that I can't hold on to anything around me? U should know that the moment U start questioning yourself indicates time where it would be recommended to step back from people and things to reevaluate U. This means initiating that one-to-one conversation with oneself and realigning your values as well as quantifying your worth. Those things in life that change automatically are date and time; we can't change people, but we can surely change ourselves. When U begin to transcend beyond who U are right now, either negatively or positively, U will find out that your crowd becomes smaller and U can call bullshit as deem fit.

See, what I was failing to do was to look at the motives and habits of others around me. If they were inactive, lackadaisical, or simply stated lazy, that means they weren't the people I needed to bond with at that moment. But at the age of 23, and as a junior in college, I didn't know how or when to do this, and more importantly, I didn't know what I was looking for. These are conversations I never had to have with my parents or anyone else. When U don't know how, U tend to continue making changes until U find a solution, right. I used to ask others the same questions that I asked myself. And I was surprised that their perspective and value concerning me was different compared to those who did me wrong. Likewise, after a while, there were still no resolutions to what was going on in my life, so I came to understand the only person who can answer what was wrong with me, was me.

Ashamed, lost, afraid, numb, but yet blessed, are the feelings I developed when I found out that I was pregnant with my son, Xavier. Although amazing, these were the hardest nine months of my life. Who would have ever thought that I was going to be something when this time came-a single Mother. I knew nothing about being a mother, and the person I associated with. Despite making the biggest mistake of my life by being with him, I received the BIGGEST BLESSING that brought me into the transition I needed in my life.

"God will push U right, when he notices the only direction U know is left!"

~ Life Coach Nesi

Gem #1:

"U don't have to accept everything thrown at U."

Are there bricks (challenges) being thrown at U at the moment?

What are they?

1

2.

3.

How are U catching them to break them down?

_____
_____
_____
_____
_____
_____
_____
_____

2

The Blessing

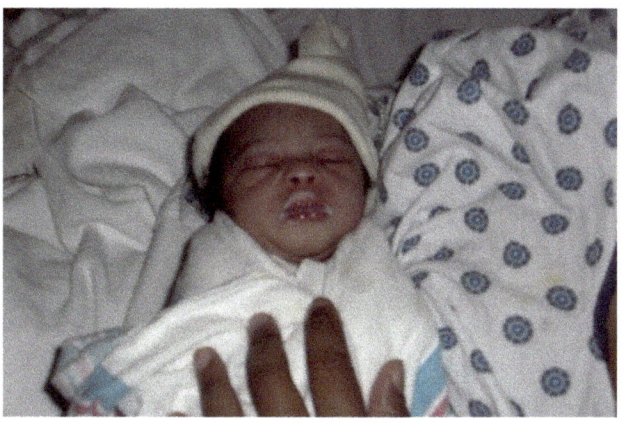

Being a mother is not an easy task, and even today I struggle with just making decisions that are in the best interest of my son. When he was smaller, I used to think about how my mother raised me and had to ask myself, what would my mother do? Quite often than none, my goal as a mother was to ensure that I gave him everything he needed, wanted (if he worked hard for it), and protect his mind and heart from the outside with knowledge and understanding. I know and acknowledge that as a woman I cannot teach a boy how to be a man; but what I can do is to show him how to treat a lady by how he treats his mother, grandmother, and great-grandmother; and place the right male role models in his life: God, my husband, coaches, mentors, my father, and brother, and be the example that I want to see in him.

U cannot force anyone to be accountable for their actions unless they choose to. What a lesson to learn after pregnancy right? Lol. Well, it was worth it. Over the course of the years, I realized a man who wants to be in his child's life will! There will be no excuses, no questions, and no lack of support (financial or physical). A person is going to do for those they choose, and that holds true for most things. Never allow anyone to tell U that U are wrong for keeping someone accountable for their wrongdoings. As a mother, it was my job to ensure that I protected the welfare of my child and I did, and was told that I was wrong! I was selfish and I was money hungry!

Being held accountable can be a hard pill to swallow, but U must be the bigger person to show that there is no challenge or situation bigger than the strength that God gave U. When U figure that out, nothing and no one else matters despite their 'lack of'! People will treat U any way that U allow and how long U allow it for!

Picture it, late June 2007 a pregnant woman sitting on her bed organizing school papers, eating Jamaican jerk chicken with rice and pea, plantain, spicy greens, drinking ginger beer, and talking on the phone. Her stomach began to hurt, and she ran to the bathroom. She was cramping on the toilet and felt something "pop!" and unable to stop using the bathroom. She noticed something red, and she became scared. She called a few friends and family members, and she began to worry that something was wrong with the baby. She panicked, and she called someone to come pick her up. Afraid to move her friend forced her into clothes other than a gown because she wanted her to look decent, despite the pain. She was pissed with her choice of whom she could have called but just happy someone was there. She left the house with baby-bag, phone, insurance card, purse and hurting like hell. She got to the hospital and expressed her thoughts about possibly being in labor or something was wrong with the baby. Nurses checked her and immediately sent her back to the see the doctor. Being one centimeter (cm) dilated, the doctor informed it was only Braxton hick's contractions, the baby was doing well. The doctor decided to keep her for a few hours more to ensure she was not entering active labor. Within two hours the doctors checked again and only one additional centimeter more. Contractions got closer, and the pain got worse. The doctor ordered the epidural because she bruised one of the nurses' hands by squeezing it so tightly despite her immediate decline. LOL I had to apologize to this nurse, she wasn't expecting me to be so strong.

After five hours of contractions she was now 8-10 cm dilated the anesthesiologist prepped for the epidural while listening to her weep and cry about fear of the effects on the baby by the anesthesia. Within a few minutes, she felt something moving in between her legs but couldn't move. She repeated she had to go "poo," and the anesthesiologist reassured it was pressure from the baby. Epidural completed, he rolled her over, and he saw the baby boy with his head already out. Immediately, the anesthesiologist called for back-up, and on June 23, 2007, in Henrico, VA, my son was delivered weighing 5lbs 4oz and 18 inches long, very little. He wasn't due until July 4th. At the time the person who brought me to the hospital and my ex (lol) were out to breakfast at the Waffle House during delivery. The epidural kicked in after giving birth, all I knew was that my biggest blessing had finally arrived.

I was showered with lovely people, mom, dad, grandmother, friends, and such an amazing hospital staff. I had so many visitors and people saying "Nesi, if U need me call me or text me; I am here for U." U know as I had that feeling of refreshment that I had people in my corner, eventually they faded away and I was left with limited resources which hurt like hell. When U give so much of yourself to others, U hope that they would do the same for U; realizing that wasn't the case was very troubling. I had a few supportive friends Jermora, Danny, Ash, Ms. Turner, My Soror, Tee, Jon Jon & DT that stood by me through most of it; if not all the shenanigans that occurred. They prayed for me, they cried with me, and most of all, they never allowed me to be alone. They allowed me to cry when I needed and free my mind of stress and fear.

I found myself depressed and lost in the year of 2007. I began to break mentally, became tapped out from disappointment after disappointment. I had the greatest blessing ever, and I didn't know what was next. I was in my senior year, and I had a newborn son. My blessing was born; I remember like it was yesterday. He was so tiny. Within in a few hours after his birth, I had to make immediate decisions about how I was going to move forward. In that year alone I had lost friends, relationships, my home, and educational opportunities, my son was all I had to keep me going. In efforts to keep it together, I was asking countless people to watch my son while I worked overnight. I had to take him to class with me because I couldn't afford daycare and I was barely sleeping. I was tired and at times the people helping really didn't want to help, my baby didn't deserve this. NONE OF IT.

I made too many attempts to contact his father, but he ignored me. No calls no nothing, and it drained me because although I made it very clear I didn't want him; I didn't want my son to be without his birth father. I was making an effort to ensure I did all I could to include him, despite his constant denial of my son. I wanted to know why he denied my boy, why he told everyone I had been with other men knowing I had only been with him, why did he lie to his parents, why he denied even being friends with me; was I that bad of a person? I did nothing to him; wait I did, I made him responsible...

I must admit I wanted to know more than wanting him a part of my sons' life. It was obvious he didn't care. I gave up on the idea that he would ever come around. I stop caring. But a wise woman told me to remember that a woman never forgets how a man made her feel during a time when she needed his support the most...It will come a day where he will need U before U need him again...lesson learned

"Sometimes it is best to let go and let God."
~ Life Coach Nesi

Late one night I walked into a grocery store and walked down the aisles figuring out what I was going to get for Xavier as he was crying and hungry. I carried my purse, his baby bag, and him in my arms. As I strolled through, tears began to roll down my face. I only had 30 cents to my name, and I knew what I had planned to do wasn't going to be right, but my baby needed food. I had not eaten in three days, but that was the least of my worries. I didn't have anyone besides my mother and father, and they were in another state.

As I cried, a lady asked me if I was okay. I was startled with fear that she knew my plan. When I responded that we were okay, she simply looked at me knowing I wasn't. As I proceed to the next aisle, I saw her again, and she approached me placing her hand on my baby's back and said, "I don't know your situation, but what U are thinking about doing, U don't have to. U don't seem like the type, and I know this because my spirit has told me. I need U to grab a cart and get what U need to last U until your next payday if U have a job; if not at least for the next two weeks." In shock, I stood there crying as she held me and told me things were going to be okay. She saw favor over my life and prayed for my baby. She bought $150.00 worth of groceries for Xavier and me and told me to thank God for my blessing. She told me to walk out and do not look back. Somewhat nervous, when I turned around she was gone. I didn't see a car leave the parking lot or anyone inside the store. What just happened?

Sometimes people see things in U that U don't see in yourself. Have faith that U can overcome your circumstances and just wait; your time is coming.
~ Life Coach Nesi

"Mommy, Zay will not stop crying." "Baby, have U fed him?" "Yes, mom I have." "Have U changed his diaper?" "Yes, mom I have." "Have U tried playing with him, laying him down, giving him a warm bath?" "Yes, mom I have tried all those things, and he won't stop! I have an organic chemistry exam in the morning mom; I can't fail this class. I can't do this anymore; I don't think I am cut out to be a mother." "Calm down baby; all new mothers go through this. He is just cranky and can't tell U what's wrong; be patient he will calm down." Later at 3:00 am, "Mom, he is still crying I can't, please help me mommy I can't do this anymore!" By 6:00 am my mother and father were at my door, and as my dad saw I had not been sleeping, he took my baby boy out of my arms while my mother packed his clothes. I didn't know what was going on; by this time I was in tears myself. My mother looked at me and said "the first time I see U slacking on your goals and school, U will come and get him and figure this out yourself. We are doing this so U can make a better life for him because he deserves it. He is still your responsibility, and U are still his mom. We are here to help U because we love U and I be damned if U do not finish school with honors. Do U understand?" Crying tremendously, I nodded. As she walked away with his items and my father followed, they headed back to North Carolina with my baby; the best decision of my life.

No more carrying my baby to class with me and standing outside of the class rocking him and taking notes on his stroller. No more asking Ms. Turner to keep him in the Hendo while I go to class. No more late fees on daycares that I could not afford. No more wondering how I was going to feed him at night. The struggle was real, but I embraced every one because I knew he had only me to depend on.

On January 21, 2009, I lost my best friend Shawn to suicide. Damn, it seemed like I couldn't catch a break! In December 2008, I had received a call, and he called me asking if I wanted to ride down to NC with him to see our last unit off to Egypt. For many years being in the National Guard, we all had the desire to go on this mission. The experience I heard was overwhelming and rewarding. I was so busy with my son, school, and trying to stay focused I had to decline. We often talked through yahoo messenger (that makes me sound so old), but when he was teaching, he would randomly vent on how frustrating his students were at that moment. He loved being a teacher. His happiness came from teaching, watching young teens mature, and giving back to the community. I loved this about him.

Shawn and I deployed to Iraq together during the first year of my military career. We became friends from the moment I met him. He was funny, and I would laugh at his lame jokes. He told me that he wouldn't talk to people if they didn't laugh at them. He was different in personality and lifestyle. He was confident in his skin and not afraid to talk about who was and what he liked. I was proud to know him and call him my best friend.

Regularly, I, would call him and check on him but now that my son was here our time had been cut short and less flexible. Being a single mother, student, full-time employee, most days I was just trying to keep up with me. I felt that no matter how much I wanted to, there were not enough hours in the day. A few months prior, he would often ask to talk, more than normal to get some things off his chest and I would promise that I'd call back and wouldn't. I would be so exhausted at times I couldn't remember what day it was. On the 19th day of January, I got the opportunity to message him back late, but I found this message in my yahoo messenger:

"Hopkins, I love U always. U have been one of the greatest individuals in my life that I met and I want U to know that I will always care for U. Know I will always love U and be there for U. Know that I will miss U."
~ S. S

In my head, I was trying to understand; where was he going? I was like okay maybe he was taking a vacation. I didn't understand. Later the next day my home girl hit me up on Facebook, and my deepest fears came to the truth. She asked me if I knew that my best friend committed suicide on the same day I messaged him. He was found with nothing in his house except his computer and gun.

I had let my best friend down being so busy with life. I was so wrapped up in my troubles that I didn't take a moment to do a five-minute check-in. I still feel myself at fault for not being there. I believe if we were friends no matter what, if U call me I need to be there. Who knows if I would have spared his life even if it was for one day to hear what was going on in his head? I don't know why he did it and I am not sure if I want to know. The story of his life will never be understood by his daughter and has been left a mystery to those who loved him so much to include me. A responsibility in which I know at times may be impossible, but willing to try my damnedest to uphold.

It is important to not forget who may be going through just as much as U are when U look to your left and right. We tend to have blinders on when challenges arouse which isn't fair to those who have been there before and didn't let U down. I hurt every day, and I promised to make him proud of me. But I vowed that no matter what, I will never put those who need me on the backburner.

He was proud of me. He told me he didn't know how I had made it through all that I had. He had given me something I had never felt from those I called friends, and that was wholeness. He was like my brother. When U begin to complain about your life, don't forget there is someone who may have it worse. Not having enough time is an excuse for U, but possibly the only time they have left. My heart bleeds when I cannot help those around me. I missed a chance to do it once; I refuse to let it happen again.

As life continued to hand me lemons, disappointment was still rearing its ugly head. I had fallen in love with someone who was different but the same as I. I knew it wasn't acceptable socially but the love was true, and it was kind. I couldn't imagine my life without them at the time. I am not ashamed of it nor do I regret it because it led me to find where I was hiding. This, someone, was there for me in many of the rough times of pregnancy and post-partum, but there were more trials and tribulations than great times to remember to include another life living with domestic violence.

When I graduated from Virginia Union University in May 2009, I graduated with a half-closed black eye. My ex punched me because I asked a question about who they were texting at 3 am in the morning on our way back from a weekend that was so good. I knew it was another female so I threw the phone. I had never felt so betrayed. They turned and punched me as I scratched and punched back. The hitting stopped when they realized my eye was closed shut.

I was being cheated on. Over the years I had to fight their jealous ex's, being disrespected in public, and I was being good to them. I had to tell many that a bee stung me and I was embarrassed. Someone I loved hit me and the fact that I had to lie to my parents didn't sit well with me. Love isn't supposed to hurt. Love isn't something one should be afraid of. But I was.

This time understanding what had occurred over the years wasn't an option; it was a must. The last four years were a roller coaster I had to get off. I was either going to jump off or it was going to crash and burn.

"The journey of a thousand miles begins with one step."

~ Lao Tzu

Gem #2:

"U have to take care of U before U can take care of anyone and anything else."

Are the bricks being thrown at U preventing U from being the best parent to your child (children)?

Why are U allowing them to block your blessings?

_____
_____
_____
_____
_____
_____
_____
_____
_____
_____
_____

3

Processes to Success

Understand Change Is a must

Of course, I eventually packed my things and left that relationship. For a while, I didn't think I could go on. I thought I couldn't do without them. I was going back down a road I didn't want to so I kept my eyes forward and didn't look back; I packed my bags and I got out.

I had a major setback in November 2009. My brother Anton passed away. I know I have not mentioned much about him, but he was my god-brother whom I had reconnected with in early 2005. When I moved out of NC, we sparingly talked; he worked, I worked but he knew I loved him. He knew that when he called, I would drop whatever I had going on for him. We had not talked in a few weeks, when I got the call from my sister that he was sick, I went into prayer immediately. Within hours, I found out while being airlifted from one hospital to the next he didn't make it and my brother was no longer here and I don't even know how. He wasn't sick when I spoke with him a few weeks ago. My heart was crushed.

Damn! U know pain is such a vicious cycle. I was over and done with life. The only thing I could do was attach myself to the bottle again to drown my pain. I started drinking "Ever clear" and "Hennessey" again. I didn't shower, clean, or eat for about a week. I was lost. I lost my best friend in January before graduation, I lost my aunt in August, and I lost my brother in November; all in one year. How do I go on? Do I? Why is God doing this to me? All I wanted to do was stay home. My mother snapped me back into reality to understand that God has a way of showing us who's God. He humbles us to remember that we are not on this earth for us but for others. We are servants, and once our job is done, he calls us home to make room for those that were born in replacement. It was the time I needed to develop a process for my success; once again.

I had many jobs to make ends meet, but that wasn't enough for me. I have never enjoyed living bare minimum. I wanted more, I needed more, so I volunteered for a deployment overseas. I was approved for the deployment, and off to Iraq again; this time I didn't mind. I understood I had to make some sacrifices to get on my feet, put some money away, and pay up the bills that I had gotten behind on. I tell U, it is so easy to get behind in bills and the hardest to catch them up.

The unit I deployed with was a unique unit I will say as it was mostly men and many of them had known each other for some time. Those that knew me knew that I was a no-nonsense, Non-commissioned officer and had a low tolerance for slackers and poor leadership; I had a mouth and wasn't afraid to use it which make it hard for me because I wanted fairness none if not for all.

Identify self

I had experienced so much pettiness that it became frustrating. Trying my hand at relationships again, I ended up being with someone that needed me, more than wanted me and he wasn't ready for what I was looking for. He played me like the iPod he used to listen to when working out. I fell for the green eyes, deep voice, and funny character but his intentions weren't good, and after about five months I slowly moved away from him realizing he was another bad decision made.

Have U noticed that I am still in search for who I am? Have U noticed that I was still seeking validation from others while not knowing what I needed validated? I had some serious self-esteem issues and no sense of direction as a mother or a woman. Although it seemed I was wrapped tight on the outside; I was a complete mess in the inside. I needed to take time for myself and that was obvious, hell it has been obvious.

I decided not to get involved with anyone else after him. That rollercoaster was enough and I knew that I could not go back down that road. Bad experiences and bad decisions were not going to get me any closer to success. He wasn't good for me and after a while one gets tired of looking stupid. It is common we want things that we know aren't what we need. He was a set up for a setback and I told myself that if I wanted someone to respect me, I had to respect myself enough to demand it; and if I wasn't getting it in the beginning cut it off right then and there. Again, I can't keep holding on to something and someone if they aren't holding me as well. Let it go!

I used to think that the worst thing in life was to end up alone. It's not. The worst thing in life is to end up with people who make you feel alone.
~Robin Williams

Identify purpose

While in Iraq I had the opportunity to help some soldiers pass the APFT (Army Physical Fitness Test). During other deployments, because it was so hot outside, the government didn't allow us to conduct outside PT. My soldiers told me they were struggling and I know how hard it can be in hot weather to train. I ran into a spin instructor who was getting ready to head back to the states and needed someone to take his spot. He did on the job training with me and just like that I was a spin instructor. I taught classes 3-4xs a week in the evenings at the MWR tent.

I loved what I was doing. Teaching came so naturally. It not only got my soldiers in shape, but I had fun doing it. If I am like most, I stayed away from the class because the seats tortured my bottom.

After 90 days of teaching, one of my soldiers said SFC Hopkins U are one excellent instructor. U should think about becoming a personal trainer. I laughed so hard, as I hated personal trainers. I thought they were a bunch of flukes; people who were in it for the money and chose google as their source of education. I was not a fan. As time drew down, more and more people were offering accolades of how talented I was and that I should consider this field because of my gift of motivation. My purpose to many of them was for the motivation to stay dedicated, disciplined, and determined; to stay consistent with working out to maintain the results they had gotten while working out with me. Also, many soldiers knew if they failed their next APFT they could be chaptered out of the military.

Before I pursued my certification, I was discouraged by seeing what I was doing as mere entertainment. My Commander and First Sergeant at the time refused to note the many improvements soldiers made on my Non-Commissioned Officer Evaluation Report! This crushed my self-esteem. Before deployment, the PT passing rate wasn't even 50% of the unit. By the time the PT test came up overseas, we were at 70% passing rate. They told me it was a choice to help them and as an NCO that is what I am supposed to do anyway. These were not my soldiers. I had no one under me, and despite the disregard, I moved on and got my certification online and went home to intern at Gold's Gym in Virginia.

I had to remember, I wasn't doing this for the accolades and if those soldiers passed their PT test, I know that I was an impact to them. Be the change that U want to see in the community, and that is giving back without seeking reward. Greater things come when the heart is pure and intentional.

Identify passion

I had never worked in a gym, and the way it operated was new. My team was great as they all joined in to show me the ropes and ensure I was providing the best service to our clients. My mentor Eric was amazing. He took me under his wing and educated me. He gave me my first client. She came to the gym in search of someone who was willing to help her save her life. I do not think either of us knew how powerful this was going to be for my fitness career. She was 463lbs, 5'4, 6 children, and a single mother. She couldn't afford personal training, so she gave up a few things, sold a few things, and made payments because the doctor only gave her six months to live. When I heard her story, I was in awe because I didn't understand how someone so smart could allow themselves to get where she was. She knew she was unhealthy physically, mentally, emotionally, and spiritually. She wanted to give up, but because there was no one and I mean no one to take care of her kids, she said, "I have to keep going." I worked with her in the gym, and she lost about 100lbs in five months. After a while, she was unable to continue paying for membership, but outside of the gym, I provided what I could to keep her going. It felt good to help someone who needed what I had; my knowledge. She followed the programs to the exact and got the results she was looking for. This was a testimony. My confidence in this moment was on cloud nine. Have U ever had a dream bigger than yourself but not imagine how big it could become?

    Eric said to me that I should start my own business because of how he has seen my work with the young lady. He saw that I was eager to research her issues and learn how to fix them holistically. He was impressed at my research methods and recommendations more than anything that worked. I thought about it, I prayed about it, and I jumped into it.

*Never say what U can't do,
if U have never done it.*

~ Life Coach Nesi

Gem #3:

"U can't give someone a broken glass."

Are U willing to pick up the pieces of your broken glass, How?

_____
_____
_____
_____
_____
_____
_____
_____
_____
_____
_____
_____
_____

4

All U Need is '1' Chance

Beginning the race

"Are U seeking ways to lose weight and get summer ready? If so, come join Get Right Fitness Bootcamp for all your health needs to get right." Oh, that was corny as hell! I knew absolutely nothing about business, liability, nutrition, or marketing, but I jumped head first. I was hoping that along the way that I could learn best business practices and strategies as I went, which eventually I found out it is the worst way to run a business and the easiest way to fail. But I had to begins this race, even if I didn't know where I was going. This was the beginning of a dream I had not yet dreamed of that was going to come true.

1 CHANCE

Have U ever sat back and thought about that one chance U didn't capitalize on, and now U realize it could have changed your entire lifestyle? I hope that right now U say yes, I do remember one situation. Were U ever afraid of failing? Were U afraid of change? Yes, that was me too. Now that I have started Get Right Fitness Boot camp, I had begun advertising through social media. I used Facebook as my main source.

U know, to be honest, I thought that I was going to have people e-mailing me day in and day out for my services because I saw everyone else having 10-15 people at their boot camps and had clientele every day. I needed the money. Coming back from Iraq, I didn't have a lot of money saved. I paid off most of my bills so that I could start with a clean slate. I had applied for jobs, but no one called not even for an interview besides Golds Gym.

In my mind, all I needed was one chance to make this right and show people what I could do. I had past athletic experience, and I had a degree. My mentor made it real clear that no one cares if I had a degree or not, they wanted to see the results I could produce. There are some doctors who can prescribe medicine all day long that only suppress the issue; we are about results and getting rid of the weight and teaching others to know how to keep it off. His life experiences and this truth started turning my thought wheels.

1 WEIGHT

What weight are U carrying on your shoulder that is preventing U from just DOING IT? What burdens are U carrying? How heavy is your load or what U think is holding U down?

My studies showed me that weights are nothing if U can't handle your own body weight and eat right. High-Intensity Interval Training (HIIT) forced me to become more in tune with my body and developing ways to help others do the same. The weight was a symbol that I didn't need much to be successful. Learn to use what I've got to make my situation work.

I didn't have much money in starting this business and couldn't afford the equipment. My very first weight was a 5lb weight from 'five and below' discount store. They sell everything U can think of, a trendy store I would say. I had to get creative with my workouts with what I had. If U know anything about this program U don't need a lot of heavyweights, 5lbs is enough to do what U need and get a good burn, especially for beginners.

1 CLIENT

All I needed was one person to help take back their life. When I left Golds Gym, my first "Get Right" client was a beautician named Steph and her mom. They were my first chance to show someone what I knew and what I could do. I started training Steph and her mom in my living room at $35.00 a month. I had to ask myself "how could I charge someone anything higher when I am working in my house or whenever the weather permits outside?" We would go to parks, sometimes I would send them to the gym with a workout I put together, and I was all over the place, but wherever I went, they did too. I must say that I appreciated that more than anything because they never complained. They would call and be ready to meet me wherever.

I saw what I was doing had some effect because both were losing weight and more people started to become interested. I disappointed a few because I didn't have a location and my services started off very crappy. I have seen how many entrepreneurs go through a dry spell and get discouraged and fall off the wagon. This made me lose sight of the reason I even got into fitness. Guess what I did eventually? U guessed it, I let everything go. I contacted all clients and informed them that Get Right Fitness Bootcamp was out of business.

This hurt my pride so much as I had never let anything shut me down. Have U ever decided on something that U didn't want to do but it was in the best interest of U? For a long time, I had to chase finances instead of my dream. I was going more and more into debt, no clients, no motivation, and depression was finding its way back. My previous clients were rooting for me. They motivated me with encouragement, praise, and kindness & understanding. They knew that I had great potential to take this business to the next level and be successful. The problem is I didn't think so. I did exactly what I told myself I wouldn't do, and gave up.

I thought I was doing well when I moved into a smaller rural area called Chester. I had a small townhome that was pink that I was renting from a slum lord but it was good, where my baby and I could walk to school, his football practice was across the street, and for a while things were complete. My beautiful mother even came to stay as she was always a support system for me; being that I was on Active Duty. It felt great to be in a position that I could support my son, pay my bills on time, and give back to those who supported me. I was finally getting ahead.

While on Active Duty, I started up a morning fitness boot camp to help increase the soldiers' physical fitness. The program was designed to bring awareness to the importance of health and wellness even while being in the Army. It became the talk of the base. I slowly gained my mojo back. In 2009 I witnessed one of the most amazing markings of history, the first African-American President, Barack Hussein Obama. What a proud moment in my lifetime. President Obama and First Lady Michelle Obama had changed the world in one night. This mark in history made me feel that anything was possible and my time was coming.

Because of such a mark in history, it wasn't too long after that the Congress started to combat the changes President Obama wanted to make in regards to the country's budget. If anyone knows anything about politics, whatever happens in Congress affects the Federal Government and can easily shut it down until resolved. Well, that is exactly what happened. The Federal Government shut down, and all soldiers and federal technicians stopped getting paid. For about two weeks we were out of work, and I panicked. What was I going to do? I was in jeopardy of losing everything that I had worked so hard to recover. I was tired of taking two steps forward only to be pushed back three.

Have U ever failed a course or dropped out because U knew it may have been too hard? When all of this was going on, I was in school at Walden University getting my Masters in Social Work. I believed this is what I wanted to do at that time and I was a year from graduating. For work I would get up in the morning at 5:00am and get my son up to take him to the babysitter, rush to a parking lot about 15 minutes away from my house to catch a van to save on gas and if U were not there on time it would leave U. Work was about 45 minutes away in both directions from home and the drive was exhausting especially during the morning. The only problem with this is when Xavier got sick at school, I had no one to get him home so this van option only worked for so long.

After getting off at 5:00pm every day, I would get home close to 6:30pm and cook dinner, talk with Xavier about his day, do homework with him, and get ready to do it all over again. I was tired. It took more out of me than I realized and all the while school suffered. I would say to myself "I will do it tomorrow," and the tomorrows turned into the next week, points taken off and grade suffering. I was taking three classes and the administrative office was not understanding at all. I explained my situation and that I was willing to put in the work to get my grades up after failing two classes. Because I did not have the GPA I was dismissed from the program and I started feeling sorry for myself. I have never failed out of a program, quit a job or activity, there was nothing I could do. I failed that's all I knew.

I moved to Northern Virginia when I received an offer from a friend to be the house manager of a newly established group home. Prior to moving my son was old enough to tell me he didn't want to move there with me. My mother, being the strong woman she was, packed up my apartment, cleaned everything and helped me move the majority of my items into storage. I understood as a new place, new people, and another change would only make things worse. My son said "mommy can I stay with big mama?" and as hard as a choice it was to make, I had to do what was in the best interest of my child; my son was gone again. During my senior year of college, I had to send him to my mother's house because I was struggling, I left for deployment which kept him at my mom's, and because of the move he was still going to stay there. I started to feel useless as a mother.

I've seen how families- mine or anyone else's can be destroyed by people taking advantage of the help they are given. Whether it was leaving children with family or borrowing money after they have used theirs for doing what they wanted and now are behind in bills. I didn't want my mother and father to feel as if I wasn't taking up my responsibility. They knew I wanted better for my son; but how can I when I can't even provide a stable home?

After my arrival, I started working at the group home and what a travesty it was. I was working for a boss who didn't care about anyone else except the money that was coming in. I stayed there as long as I could bare her attitude. The final straw was when one of my soldiers committed suicide that I needed to be there; she politely said, "U are a National Guard soldier. When U are off work, U work for me, and on your weekends, U work for them. Don't use my time to do their work!" She was a retired military officer; that made it even worse. I attempted to restart my fitness business with no name at the time, and I heard more often than I would like, "Prices are too high, I can't afford U," "can I do a payment plan," and never receive payments. I was frustrated and annoyed by the excuses. I looked at myself one day and said Nesi; U must uncover the new U! U have been doing the same thing for so long and are continuing to get the same results. Why are U settling on yourself? U are your biggest enemy!

I realized then that no amount of money would allow me to stay and work for such a person. I was better than that and had more to offer. I quickly exited the stage and left when I got the offer for a three-month tour at the National Guard Bureau (NGB).

How long will U continue doing the same things in life that keep U in the same place? It is time to move out of YOUR own way.

~ Life Coach Nesi

Gem #4:

"U cannot have something U are not willing to work for."

What scares U about change if anything?

1. _____
_____
_____
_____
_____

2. _____
_____
_____
_____
_____

3. _____
_____
_____
_____
_____

5

Change Your Mind
Change Your Circumstance

Dedication is something I said I needed but is hard to hold on to. If I felt that I was going to fail at something, I would stop the entire process to understand what's wrong then start again, which is not always a good thing for a business. Once I grasped it, I held on to it. I had to understand why consistency was an important piece of the fitness lifestyle and how to demonstrate and teach how it works. While working at NGB, my mind wasn't on fitness; rather, it was on landing an Active Guard Reserve position (AGR), which would put me on active duty for a minimum of 3 years. Many people didn't stay around too long because most of the staff were high profile officers such as one and two-star Generals and can be hard to work for. I knew I was qualified. Everything at NGB was based on funding and rank. In the areas I worked they did not have any funding to support my rank at the time. I did, however, find another location that did and landed a one year tour in recruiting and retention.

I was starting over, but I didn't mind. I was back on the right track and moving in the right direction. That meant bills were getting paid on time, could do more for my son, and invest a little into me among many other things. I had a steady job, and my mind was focused on improvement. I was diligent in my studies of fitness and wanted to upgrade my status. I paid for my certification as a Master Fitness Trainer which would allow me legally to offer more to future clients. This wasn't easy as I worked full time, and the traveling back and forth to work was overwhelming due to the horrendous traffic. I would get off work at four and most days arrive back at home by seven or eight. I still managed to get it done and completed, but it was rough.

I was in the gym every morning. It was of huge benefit to get there early as I could get a great parking spot LOL. Over time, I made many connections and received quite a few inquiries about personal training. Chief was one of my first clients, and he was amazing! He became my mentor in the process, and I helped him lose over 30lbs. He increased his PT score, and he was eating so much better. His sense of humor, dedication to my program, and positive attitude jump-started my motivation once more, and that helped me get back into the personal training business. I was dedicated this time to making this work.

Discipline proves if U can stick to one thing for a long period without quitting, U tend to be successful as U continue to progress. So, this time I wasn't giving up. I stuck to my regiment and training my one client, but little did I know that someone was watching the discipline I had towards him. Late one afternoon, I received an email message from someone who said they wanted to speak with me in regards to training. Never had I met her, seen her, or heard of her. And the first thing that came to my mind was I had done something wrong, and someone was going to reprimand me. We, however, met during our lunch period, and her first words were, "I've been trying to find U for the longest." She went on to tell me that she was a two-time breast cancer survivor twenty years apart and had been through so much mentally, emotionally, physically, and spiritually. She discussed some personal things with me that made me felt stronger for her instead of feeling sorry. Her only objective was to continue living and get back to who she was physically & emotionally. Chemotherapy had taken so much of her life, and she wanted it back.

Do U have any idea how heavy this request was for me? I had never worked with anyone who had such a disease. Yeah, high blood pressure, thyroid issues as well depression clients are tough to manage and monitor in fitness, but breast cancer? Do I turn this opportunity down or go for it? With the numerous questions flooding my mind on whether I could handle this or not, I had to ask why me. She said, "why not U? I see U with Chief, and he has amazing results and look at U, your body is GREAT LOL. I want to give U a try if U can." With the eagerness to get started, I said 'Yes' without hesitation.

Determination

I was dedicated to learning all about breast cancer and how to change, the body after it had been chemically altered. Knowing I had to manage every component of her body, I went back into medical books and also invested in medical journal sites. Likewise, I made deep researches on the diverse programs that have helped past breast cancer patients and have equally improved their overall being. This was an opportunity to help this Queen take back her life! I appreciated being an in-home trainer, because she was comfortable in her space. And because this is how all of this came to be, I was an expert at knowing what it took to train at home and gain results.

When I arrived, her husband was all over me with questions and wanted answers. I was psyched because he wanted to know how I was going to help her, what was my plan, did I know what I was doing, and he made sure I knew he was there as her support system from start to finish. Now if I didn't have thick skin, I would have felt quite intimidated by this man Lol. I never encountered someone who was so supportive of his spouse and also engaged in their transformation process. I made sure that when I spoke, I spoke with knowledge and accuracy, to gain the respect and trust regarding anyone's health, there must be accountability, accuracy, and attention, of which I provided every session. Over time, this couple became my family. They are now mom and pops! They saw my drive, they saw my determination, and they saw my desire. I wasn't giving up this time.

Tina taught me that patience is a virtue. No matter the smallest setbacks, they were always a set up for increased results. When her body gave up on me, she didn't; she came back for more with increased intensity. I got used to the screaming at me, the mad faces, and being put out on regular, Lol. It was all out of love and I just wanted her to have the results she desired. by any means necessary LOL.

Just when U think all hope is gone, something or someone changes that mindset. What is the point of giving up? Giving up only showed me that things would NEVER get better because U are not doing anything about it. So why give up! Trust me; I know that it is easier said than done, but being determined to change your circumstances pushes U one step closer to the smaller changes that eventually lead to the larger ones. It takes time and if U want it bad enough keep going for it. When was the last time U gave up on something? Do U regret doing it? Are U ready to start again?

Tina and I were together for two years with a total of 40lbs lost. Her journey alone aspired many others to get up and move! If she could do it, then anyone could. This is exactly the message I wanted everyone to hear. She was a living proof that once U take back your health everything in the inside and on the outside will change too. Tina was happier with herself and had built up the confidence she once thought she lost. She became more active, and she increased her PT scores every time after that. She learned to appreciate the small successes over large ones because it was something she had not been able to achieve five years before me.

She survived! She will forever live with the effects of what chemo did to her inside and out, and despite the many afflictions it left, she still HASN'T QUIT YET. One of the strongest women I know. She survived and so will I. Her life and what I've come to know about it says 'U can never stop fighting if U want to be the greatest version of yourself every day.' It is not about what happens to U; it is about what U do after the happenings that matter. Yes, I've struggled like hell, but that doesn't mean I quit fighting to get ahead. Find my place in this world and act on it. If U give up on U, the only person U will be hurting is yourself. For she is the reason my purpose is greater than I. For this moment everyone I was whole, I was surviving; I had 'Uncovered The New Me'.

I D.I.D it!
~ Life Coach Nesi

"Never burn the bridges U walk across, U never know when U will need to walk across them again."

~Life Coach Nesi

Gem #5:

"If U don't have a plan to develop a program for success then what is your purpose?"

What is your plan?

_____
_____
_____
_____

What is your program (how will you do it)?

_____
_____
_____

What is the purpose of your program?

_____
_____
_____
_____
_____

6

Building and Rebuilding Bridges

Name five people that U have disconnected with and write them down. Now put the reasons why U disconnected with them. Ask yourself was that a good reason to disconnect with them?

I can sometimes be stubborn as a mule, for that reason over the years I have disconnected with many people simply because of how they made me feel. I can't wait to be hurt by anyone, so if I feel uncomfortable I don't wait for an explanation I move on. As I have been hurt by many and disgusted by some, I have learned that when I am done, that means I am DONE! Time goes forward not backward, and that is the same with people and me. Despite the way I feel, it is not healthy when U do such to family and close friends. Challenges can make or break relationships, especially when U do not know how to balance them out to work through them. Growing as a person has allowed me to review my toxicology report and pull out those that were causing me to die inside. I did this quite often, but I had to learn to slow down as I removed some that were helping me heal. And that is because I realized not everyone was out to hurt me.

My brother was one of them. He was among those that I avoided BUILDING a relationship with for so long because of the relationship he had with my family and his friends. My brother and I were like night and day. He is the calm, collective, and a cool one, I am the sassy, snappy, and solid one. He handles life in such a manner that I probably could not function. He was successful in sports, people liked him, and he was popular, and I wasn't. I was jealous, and because of the jealousy, I avoided him at all cost. I didn't call as much nor did I engage in his conversation. In due time, I learned why this bridge was the one I needed. I am sure U can relate to how many siblings fight, argue, curse each other out, and even go the extra mile to betray the trust of each other. My brother and I aren't like that. We weren't raised as such either. But something my parents prided themselves on is showing us that family is all we have, and family isn't only by blood. My brother is a man who lives fruitfully day to day. He doesn't rush the process but just appreciates each day as it comes. As I grew older and began to see that was something I too needed to learn, and he and I began to fall in line. He is the other half of me to see things clearly and to see inside the box for so long I had to fight my way out of. He gave me what I needed inside, PEACE.

Family can hurt U just as much as they can help U. They can disappoint U just as much as they can make U angry. But does that change the values that U have toward one another? NO. I learned a valuable lesson from my best friend Shawn, RIP; don't wait to give the ones U love flowers when they are dead because they will never be able to see the beauty. Give them flowers while they are still alive and help them plant the seeds to make more. And for that reason, I honor my grandmother, Mamu. I have no idea where the name came from, but Xavier started calling her that, and it stuck.

While my father traveled with the military in my younger years, my mom wanted to stay close to Mamu. Mamu happened to be the matriarch of our family. Holidays, family events, and family challenges are orchestrated based on her desires and needs. It has always been that way. She was strict, and she was very adamant about behavior, attitude, and cleanliness. We got popped for not washing our hands before going into the refrigerator, popped when we talked back and popped for not brushing our teeth at night. And if she didn't smell soap on our bottoms, we had to get back in the shower to wash again. LOL. Mamu is the truth; she taught me the rules of life without leaving Xavier out of the teachings. She is a staple in my upbringing because the encouraged ways of life and mannerisms from my youth kept me together without even realizing I had put them to use.

How many of U can say that your grandmothers or grandfathers had a hand in raising your children their way? My granny was born in the late 1930's, and her way of living was doing it by hand, from scratch, and making it work with what U have. That lesson taught me to struggle and not to complain. It has been a blessing and a curse to have such a prestigious woman in my corner. The reason I say 'curse' is because as I got older, and I saw how some family members who lost their value took advantage rather than being an advantage for her. I became very protective and had to cut ties with them because of it. The power of my grandmother was a direct source of my energy; I couldn't allow that to be interrupted. Family is supposed to stick together not rip it apart..

To heal, U must also REBUILD relationships. I understand how hard it can be to forgive someone that has hurt U, but forgiveness isn't for them, it is for U. There are a lot of people who I had to eliminate because of the toxins they were producing in my life. Just as I had to learn about life, so did they. We all have had a growing pain or two, and that has formed a part of our shifting and transitioning. My Chaplain in the Army gave me a twenty-one day, Prayer Dare challenge. One of the questions stated:

"If your horizontal relationships are broken, then your vertical relationships are too. Before U talk to anyone else, go talk to the person U are not right with."

One of the stumbling blocks I found to healing in life is broken relationships. I had to look at myself and ask if I had done enough to repair them. What relationship needs is to be mended, though, not necessarily restored, but made right, for the sake of your peace within. I chose two because I knew that I could have worked through them, repair and restore what we had. TJ and my ex-roommate were never bad people but fell into bad situations that caused them to make bad decisions that affected me. I had to sit back and realize that they are human too and experience stress in the same manner as I. I am not perfect so how can I expect them to be. I am grateful that we took the time to talk and restructure what never left. Communication was the only thing missing in repairing the bridge that we all need to walk across. Time heals all wounds and I am thankful for that time. We all need that time to learn, listen, and live through challenges just like the next. We aren't perfect but as the clock circles back to twelve, so do people in our lives.

"Not everyone in your corner wants to see U win."

~ Life Coach Nesi

Gem #6:

"Not everyone in your life is out to hurt or deceive U!"

Have U ever thought about why people come in and out of your life as they do?

1._____
_____
_____
_____

2._____
_____
_____
_____

3._____
_____
_____
_____
_____

7

The Spine

MY YEAR OF COMPLETION

Support does not come easy when U are an entrepreneur. In my life, I can count on a hand in a half; the number of people that I know have poured into my business or to me. When I was pregnant, I learned that not everyone who says they will be there for U will show up. I had to learn to depend on me and my drive.

Partner in Crime

How many of U have mothers that serve as your backbone? My mother has been the backbone of my life since I was 16 years of age. The reason I said since 16 was because that was when I realized I needed her. Growing up, our parents did what they must to take care of us; that is what they are supposed to do. I didn't understand the need and desire for support until I genuinely needed my mom and without question, she was there for me. She didn't hesitate, question me nor did she ever complain about being there.

Through my journey of life, I still this day do not do anything without the approval of my mother. Why? Well because she has been my biggest cheerleader. No matter the cost, time, or sacrifice she did for me without complaint. I cannot fathom what I would do without her. Our relationship is not always the best which I am thankful for. It is in those moments that I hurt her, lashed out at her, and even disrespected her that made me appreciate all she has done for me even more. We often take for granted those who love us by hurting them and denying their sacrifices.

For all the pain U have caused others, U first must forgive yourself and understand your shortcomings or downfalls. In growing and even now as a mother, I understand most if not all of them; the struggles my mother has endured raising my brother and me. I know even more now as a wife, the reason behind the choices she made for her children. Mom, I apologize; for the pain, I have caused U through the years. It took our experiences, the tears, the days without talking, even if it was just one to open my eyes and realize that U were the making of me. U gave me what I needed to move past my pain. U are my best friend, and I could not see running this race alone.

Investor

Picture it; August 2, 2015, U were driving into a grocery store right after working out, sparked up a conversation with someone who followed U around the store, exchanged numbers in agreeance to help U train for your first competition, and on September 5, 2015, he proposed to U. Lol. In that exact order! I counted myself out after having my son that no man would ever love me being a single mother, bad credit, and a broken heart.

Let's be clear; my mindset was that as a single mother, men would want to know what I did wrong for the father of the child to leave. I heard often that a man would never leave his son especially unless something was wrong with the mother. She had to be crazy, only wanted money and didn't care about the child, or wanted him and he didn't want her; but something was definitely wrong with her. "What is wrong with me?" Thinking about the 'would have, could have, and should have' made me feel as if I had no worth to a man. When I met Mr. Ewing everything changed. He was imperfect, he was flawed, made mistakes in his life, and wanted a change just like me. He was broken inside, he was weakened by his past, and fearful that love was going to bypass him. He was incomplete just like me. But what happens when two halves come together; they become whole! U see, I took a break from men and relationships; 7 years to be precise. Little did I know that Biblically, 7 is the number of completion. I met him on the 2nd + engaged on the 5th married on the 25th, 7 was Gods intention! Hear this! God broke me all the way down. I was close to losing everything again even after being pregnant and homeless. And the moment I began to transition in my life, it was a man that was sent to me.

I had very little support in my mission to success; but when I met Mr. Ewing he invested in me; something that no man or woman relationship wise has ever done for me. He invested in getting to know me and my desires. He invested in equipment for my gym, helped me gain clientele (football players), and he took over the male responsibility of my son. He said he is now mine; he has nothing to worry about while I am here. What do U say about a man willing to accept U and all your baggage? Do U think he is ready for it? I didn't think so because the investment he was making in me came with a lot of hurt, frustration, anger, tears, FEAR, and pain.

What is even more amazing is that we love the same exact things. Sports fanatics, Dallas Cowboy lovers, Dak Prescott fans (from Mississippi State), working out, traveling, meal prepped food, the sun, family, and being loved intentionally and unconditionally. The only thing that divided us was basketball. Lol. He is a LeBron James fan I am a Steph Curry lover. I am not even sure how common it is to have almost everything similar to your spouse. Our marriage isn't perfect; whose is? What does matter is that we became one on His accord, and not on our own. I didn't look for him like I always did, he wasn't looking for me; it just happened. I invested in myself by finding me and knowing what I deserved. God revealed my worth by showing me how to love myself through Him and without regard; and when it was time, everything came to pass.

I want U to be patient in your journey of investment. People won't invest in what U have or what U are doing, they will invest in who U are. If people believe in U, no matter what U are doing they will offer any help U need. U see, a lot of my support from Mr. Ewing didn't come from the fact that he enjoyed working out neither did it come from his desire to want to see me grow. He saw it was my passion and that was all he needed to know. I had already gotten the certifications, degrees, and license. I just needed that 'one' to jump-start, to bring my dream of having my own to light.

"Blue twenty-two, blue twenty-two! Down set, hut hut!" I am on the fifty-yard line, and I've got the ball, I am headed to the end zone, I look left there is no one there, I look right there is no one there. Where are my receivers damn, I've got to just go for it! I begin to run, and I get to the forty, thirty-five, and I am knocked out of bounds." This is what it looked like when my husband left for a job in another state. I was left to train football players on my own. Being a woman who knows the game inside and out is not an easy concept for some men to grasp. I have heard some very derogatory comments about where I should be and what my job was as a woman. Ignorance is so bliss!

It is a heavy task when young men or women are depending on U to get them where they need to be to get to the next level. I know many elite athletes' parents desire them to train in large facilities that cost hundreds of dollars, and with fancy equipment. Well, Uncovering the New U, LLC was not that. I trained out of my then one car garage. I kept it warm when it needed, cool when desired, and available from 0500-2300 M-Fri and some Saturdays and Sundays. I was committed to showing my boys that U don't need all of that to become great.

Before Mr. Ewing left, there was one client who I cannot forget, and that is Jay and his father, Stan. I had four total clients, and out of my football players, he was my only quarterback to stay with me. Stan said to me, "Nesi U have something that these boys need; not just training but leadership as well. I need Jay to see those key fundamentals. Besides being in the military and working my way up through the ranks, I had never had anyone to acknowledge me as a leader. Hell! Even my leadership in the military didn't want to give me the title as I kept my soldiers accountable for their actions and wasn't going to allow myself or them to be treated just any kind of way.

Jay graduated from high school and went on to play college ball. I am still proud of his accomplishments and I hope to see him in the NFL one day along with a degree in hand. He has the dedication, discipline, and determination to do it that was taught by me and implemented on the field.

But Jay went from honorary to humble one of my biggest accomplishmmets. He learned that yes, it is an honor to be one of the best QB's in the state, but he was humbled that his father continued to invest in the ability to learn those tools to be the best QB in that period. My motto is, if U are going to tell me something, show me as well. So, for that reason, I beat the odds with working with this young man especially being the leader he needed to see outside of those he already had. Focused in school, leading the team from the front on and off the field, and giving credit where it is due. To be elite, U must uncover new traits within that U may not know existed; although not everyone is born a leader. U should learn how to govern and lead yourself for others to follow. For this Jay broke state records, set the standard for the upcoming QB, and left his teammates knowing what right looks like.

This investment my husband made in me was an opportunity waiting. He saw that my purpose was greater than me. As soon as others saw how I had transformed Jay, they wanted in and bought into my program. This wasn't by chance it was my one opportunity that helped in giving me the confidence I needed to always want more out of what I was doing.

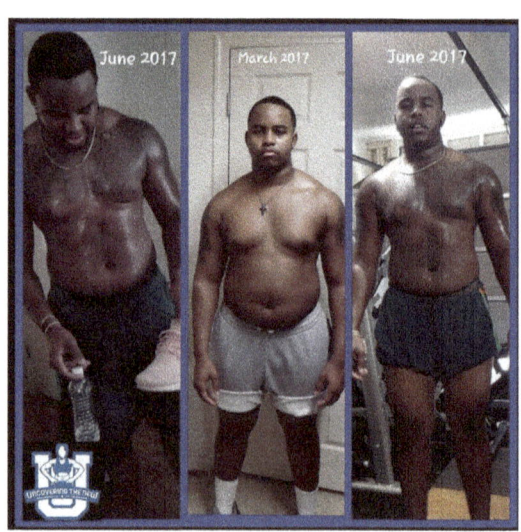

Uncle Huddy

Have U ever heard that U learn some of the most profound lessons from those U don't know than those U do know? Well, this was what I found in Hudson, aka Uncle Huddy. Uncle Huddy became more of a son than a client to me over time. His dominant personality, intelligence, standards of self and those around him, his humbleness, and his outlook on life took me beyond what I was accustomed to when working with high school football players. He was a leader from the day he stepped foot in my house and said, "I am ready!"

As I grew to know him, I had to take a step back and wonder at times if he was the adult and I was the child. And this was because as eager as I was to mentally to move forward, his process of weight loss and the balance of some other personal issues he shared heightened my awareness and forced me to be patient and allow life to happen. I was still trying to force success to happen knowing how steadfast I honestly need to be. I learned a lot about myself from Uncle Huddy. I became the leader he needed, but he was the lesson I needed. Doesn't matter the age, everyone that comes into your life will uncover something about U; either good or bad.

Jaz

"Never judge a book by its cover!" This young lady gave me a run for my money when it came to breaking down barriers of life and facing challenges that so many of us may or may not see. Her confidence alone gave me life. A strong single mother she was and this gave me the drive I needed on a personal level. She brought something to the table that I thought I would not see again; she brought a little bit of me. This pushed me to want more and do more to continue to inspire her to do the same.

My clients have highlighted a portion of me. Without them, I would never be where I am today. I often hear the term "self-made," and despite having three degrees, I would have never gained the experience to perfect my craft if it wasn't for them trusting me with their health and wellness. They allowed me to revise, reset, and realign the tools I already had, and for that, I am truly grateful.

Royalty in Blue

I am Three, a rich coffee-cake made from scratch with sugar and spice, and chopped pecans; I am Sock It to Me. I am bold yet intentional with everything that I do and an antioxidant for those around me. On December 17, 2016, BakerZ DoZen So Sweet entered into Finer WomanHood as new members of Delta Zeta Zeta Chapter of PG County, Maryland. Zeta Phi Beta Sorority, Incorporated changed my life. Each one of them brought something unique to the line and in a short amount of time these ladies were no longer friends, they became my sisters ALL 13 OF THEM. I have never had sisters before. For two years before elevating to a finer woman, there were four beautiful sisters that I grew with. We were challenged each day and year to wait our turn to join such an amazing sisterhood.

I was turned away from one because I wasn't popular enough or just didn't hang with the right people. I had to ask myself "is that the type of organization U want to be a part of?" I had to honestly say no. I had to do my research, and I am glad that I waited until I was out of undergrad because I would not have done it for the right reasons. I found that sororities can bring out the truth in people and how vain they can become. I've seen the good, the bad, and the ugly of it all. We ultimately have the same purpose just wearing different colors. But there should be a purpose behind what U are doing and what U stand for.

I crossed so many bridges in my life that I wanted to belong to something that was bigger than me. I wanted to give back to the young, millennial, and the old; be an example to women across the world. I questioned myself daily if this was for me if I would fit in, and what did I have to offer? In so many words I had to step back and say listen "U have everything to offer others just as U do yourself." My purpose once more was bigger than myself, and it wasn't about me; more about who I could help others become. There are so many who desire to be a part of a sorority and never do because of the stigmas. Which is why I am so thankful that I took my time to do my research to ensure I made the right decision.

Getting to the final point of membership was nothing other than exhausting and emotional filled with long days and long nights. There are always challenges U face with women from different backgrounds and beliefs come together. But I would not change those challenges for anything. Each of them from 1 to 13 is unique to the line we created and the number chosen for us. We are constitutionally bound and finer in the only colors we wear, Royal Blue and White. We range from young to old. Despite the age differences not one of them has an old soul and can get down when it's time. I came with them, I conquered with them, and I will succeed with them-the true meaning of sisterhood. I know I would not have found this union anywhere else. My path was lit with Zeta Light and forever will be.

"A journey is best taken with those who desire to take it with U."

~ Life Coach Nesi

Gem #7:

"People will invest in whom they believe in."

Who keeps U grounded 365 days of the year? Name your top 5:

1. _____
_____

2. _____
_____

3. _____
_____

4. _____
_____

5. _____
_____
_____

8

Nothing Stands Between U and Success But U

Trust your instincts when they occur; wrong or right. The results of what happens hold a lesson that U need to know now or later. That is how I felt when I first heard about becoming a life coach. In August 2016, I became certified as a Health and Wellness Life Coach through an amazing company called Dimensioned Wellness, LLC.

I knew nothing about life coaching as previous thoughts connected it closely to the use of therapeutic techniques. When I found out that it wasn't, I was even more excited to grasp the concept as a way of helping others balance life and health. I believe everything is intentional when U work with people and they trust your work and like what U do. My friend, mentor, Owner, and CEO of Dimensioned Wellness, LLC invited me out in July (7) 2014 to offer an amazing Stiletto Workout in Washington, DC.

The women had a fantastic time and little did I know that this was the start I needed to be complete. I was thrilled at the nuggets received from the Life Coaching School and proud to have been privy to attend such a program.

Shortly after graduating the life coaching school, I started S.H.E. Can U guess the acronyms? Yes, it is me but its Strength, Health, and Empowerment Life Coaching. My purpose is to teach others how to balance the four components of intentional living and to help them make leading a life of optimum health, not a task but simply a lifestyle. To be healthy physically, one must be healthy mentally. One should know how to handle what moves their balance scale. When thrown off one thing, another can weigh heavier on the body or mind and shift the mindset. Being able to teach others how to build their strength helps to increase their health and empower others to want to do the same.

    Believe in yourself or no one else will. How do we know that? I had to believe that I would be able to leave my mark and desire for change in the world in one way or another. I had to believe in my ability to become my hero, act on my dreams, and accept nothing less of what I deserved. Whoever said that U can't be a single mother and have dreams? Who said U had to settle for the minimum for the sake of your children or circumstances? No one!

    I started two businesses being broke, broken and bruised. I jumped into both. I didn't wait for my son to turn 18 years of age before I decided to focus on me. Why wait? My parents showed me that we when U set yourself up for success, U set your children up as well. My father did it through military, mom did it by working at a job for 20 years, and now I am doing it for my son, leaving him two businesses to grow and flourish.

Become your own hero

    Attempting to plan a wedding in 2016 I was also finishing my Masters in Sports and Health Science with a concentration in Exercise Psychology. I started my journey because I watched everyone around getting higher degrees and doing better. What made me any different? The military was paying for my schooling so what did I have to lose? It was a lot on my hands, but I managed. I told myself U must do what U want to do right now. I am a junkie for education except for math and history lol. But I was studying something so dear to my heart, sports.

I've seen so many women give up on what they wanted in life because of the stigma after we have children; it is not about us anymore it is about the children. But if we as mothers or fathers are in bad shape what can we do for the children? It can't be all about them anymore. I couldn't mask the pain it caused me to think of giving up an opportunity to be my hero and beat the odds to become a hero to my son. As the only active parent in his life, I had to show him that there is nothing that can stop U from being successful but U. When U decide to move out of your way and go for what is in your heart, it is moments like this that U can enjoy and become full from.

Currently, I am the road to obtain my Doctorate in Psychology with a concentration in Sports and Performance. I will be Class of 2019, Dr. SheNesia S. Ewing.

Fitness business was going well, and I was determined to increase my clientele in life coaching. That process was very slow. Many did not and still do not know what life coaching is all about. As I began spreading my value across the states, it is because of that determination, I was nominated and selected as Wellness Life Coach of the Year. U want to talk about a natural high! I had never won anything so prestigious, so I thank U all that voted for me. I could not have won without U.

Act

It can be very scary to move into your lane, on your path, with results that are only going to be gained by U. Not knowing the results U will receive and if it will be successful is a rough emotion. As many times as I have set out on my journey of sole entrepreneurship, I have failed. I haven't gained enough clientele to withstand doing what I love full time. The common saying if U are busy and broke, U are only running errands; but at this moment I believe that partially. I started two businesses that are popular in their way and can be presented in many ways. At this point, right now I am in my lane and driving slow to ensure I don't catch a ticket to set me back. I am acting on what I know, what works and investing in myself consistently to grow and improve. I used the money I was making on active duty to not only pay bills but to invest in my business.

I paid for my equipment out of pocket so that I would not have any more debt added to what I had. I turned my one car garage into a gym. It was small enough to hold seven clients at once and rotate as needed. I made it work!!!!!! I stayed dedicated to my dreams. And that is all it takes to gain momentum and shift in your cirucumstances.

*It ain't about how hard U hit, it's about how hard U can get hit and keep moving on.
That's how winning is done."*

~ Sylvester Stallone

Gem #8:

"BE YOUR OWN HERO!"

What is something U want to do that U just have not taken the step to?

_____
_____
_____
_____
_____
_____
_____
_____
_____
_____
_____
_____
_____
_____

9

Set Back or Set Up?

There is no amount of money that I will not spend on any lawyer to save my son. For ten years, I have given him my all; blood sweat, and tears with no complaints, no request, and seeking no handouts. No one has done that for him but me and those involved in MY life!

Mr. Ewing was offered an amazing job in Atlanta, GA and time was winding down to decide if he was going to take it or not. My command received a letter stating I had kept my son away from his father, my child was in danger, I was unfit, and if I did not respond immediately my son could be taken from me! No way in hell was I going to let this happen. I was trying to understand how someone goes from being absent for most of his life and come back attempting to take my child overnight. This was NOT HAPPENING.

I did everything I could which included spending over $10,000 from my savings to get a lawyer. This was another setback from my plan to set myself up for success. I prayed. I started saving because I knew the transition would happen this year or the next. I knew that I could not allow myself not to support Mr. Ewing in his attempt to provide a great foundation for our family. He was already holding it down, allowing me to save and maneuver; and this happened. I should admit that I was afraid I would lose him. Why? I guess because of their position in the city, and I will leave it at that. The system denied me of so much when my son was younger that when it came to my son, I can't trust the law especially knowing they are affiliated with it.

But here again I asked myself, "if U knew all the work U have put in and followed the rules, why question your ability as mother?" I had to stop for a moment and realize all the things this man has put me through, from the dishonesty to drama, and the lack of care for my son, this wasn't about him; what he put me through was what I allowed him to put me through. When U change your mind about situations, your circumstances change too. I had to get him out of my head and allow him to be in his lane with the issues he had. They weren't mine. I was not a bad mother because I pursued my dreams. I wasn't a bad mother because I had the support of my family to make a way out of no way. It has given my son lessons that he will never learn anywhere else. There is no other role model I would rather have for him than me. Society often raises children, and they either end up dead or in jail, which I refuse to let mine be a part of.

It is safe to say that my baby is still with me living his best life. Growing, getting older, and running me ragged lol. The situations that came before relocation are those that made it clear that the chapter had been closed. What happened then will not happen again because I have made the necessary moves to ensure that it will not. It is in those lessons of life that we find who we are and what we can hold on too. I wish I could tell U that this journey is easy but it is an emotional rollercoaster and I am rooting for U. Stay the course because your breakthrough is coming.

I thought going through that was enough to deal with until I found myself giving more of me than I had to give to an old friend. She brought energy that I should have never accepted into my life AGAIN that almost cost me my relationship with my husband and children. I was allowing things to occur that should not have been, because she was supposed to be my "friend." She was a setback emotionally especially in this moment because she was comfortable being STUCK in her ways of life as I was outwardly growing. There was always an excuse of why she can't and she was setting herself back by the lies she told herself and the alcohol she was abusing, just the old version of me. I came out of my element and turned in to someone that I was unwilling to be, and that was hateful and angry. When U know that someone is setting U back to your old ways of life when U had nothing, that is a sign that U must move them out of your way. It is okay to outgrow people U love and care about. If they are not willing to go the distance with U or support U from afar, then they are not meant to travel with U. U cannot let them set up for a setback. When all has been said and done I am okay that we will never be friends again, but it hurts to see such a talent wasted on excuses.

Before I left Virginia, I applied to write in a magazine by life coaches (The Life Coach Network Magazine). This was an amazing opportunity because as many health and wellness coaches are amongst us, she chose me for the opportunity.

I applied to attend an International Retreat shortly after to be held in United Emirates, Dubai. I WAS SELECTED. U are now looking at International and Award Winning Life Coach Nesi. I am overjoyed how no matter how far I was set back; my success wasn't altered. To be selected for this opportunity was something grand, she could have chosen anyone, but she chose me.

I have always wanted to go to Dubai, and this experience taught me about worth and opportunity. If U know your worth, others will not attempt to lower it by asking for cheaper prices. They will take advantage of the opportunities U possess and capitalize on them. Success looks different in everyone's eyes, and we cannot dim the light of those who are making strides forward faster or slower than the next. Celebrate the success of those around

U; it is good for the soul and your character. There is nothing wrong with watching another Queen rise.

I do not take selections like this lightly as these opportunities began to open a plethora of podcast interviews, becoming a contributor to a book, and public visualization which I am thankful for. Especially times like this when I am humbled by opportunity rather than things happening by chance.

Gem #9:

"Never let anyone doubt your ability as a MOTHER or woman!"

What are the TOP 5 reasons U chose to become a mother?

1. _____
   _____

2. _____
   _____

3. _____
   _____

4. _____
   _____

5. _____
   _____
   _____

10

Change Begins With U

I cannot stress enough how your life is based on how U react to the situations within it. If U want something out of life, no one can take that opportunity from U no matter your circumstances. Believe in who U are, what U are doing and whom U are doing it for. Nothing is more powerful than the strength within.

I could have given up years ago. I could have thrown in the towel and allowed life to happen without regard. But I decided it was time for me to stand up and face life because for so long I was letting life run me and that is vice versa. Uncovering the new U is all about uncovering the person U have always desired to be and living your best self intentionally. Are U happy mentally? Are U happy emotionally? Are U happy physically? Are U happy spiritually? If U are not, think about ways U can change those circumstances to become happy. Happiness is in the eye of the beholder. If U aren't healthy, U won't be happy being wealthy. If U aren't wealthy, U won't be happy being healthy. I know it sounds cliché, but it is true. U can find happiness if U desire to find it.

I know U wonder what makes me so qualified to say these things. Well, because I lived it. I went through the stages of life where I wanted to give up and call it quits, but guess what? I still have setbacks and I still struggle. The biggest difference now than then is that I know how to deal with those challenges to ensure they don't destroy me. I think we all have seen what struggle looks like at some point in our lives. Right? But I chose to change my mind to change my circumstances. I chose to make the efforts needed to protect my mind, spirit and most of all my son.

Every day that I look into my sons' eyes, I think of the challenges that he has ahead being a young man in today's society. I vowed to teach him the lessons of life that will make him a better man. And as he learns from those lessons, I will also show him how to remain balanced as he gets older and the challenges begin to increase. The sacrifices are at times gut wrenching but the faith I hold in myself keeps me grounded and my steps in order.

Be intentional about the moves U make in life going forward. We may not have the power to change what our past looks like but we can turn the light on in the path going forward. Don't ever look back; there is nothing there. Always be the best version of U and never settle for the lesser of two evils.

"Down set hut hut!" I've got the ball I am on the fifty-yard line, and I am almost to the endzone, just keep running and don't look back, I am at the 70-yard line, please block for me, here we go, we are in! TOUCH DOWN!!!!

U HAVE WON!

LET'S WERK

These are the steps I took to change my mind to change my circumstances.

1. Identify Self
2. Identify purpose
3. Identify Passion
4. Dedication, Discipline, and Determination (DID)
5. Trust
6. Believe
7. ACT

Strength Health Empowerment Offers A 7-Week Empowerment Course On Specific Areas Of Life Delivered By Life Coach Nesi, Empowerment Coach In Person & Online.

Each course includes solution oriented empowerment techniques, life skills, & empowerment to find self.

Module 1: Finding U

- Accept where U are
- Removing Roadblocks/ Letting Go of Past
- Self-Reflection

This course helps in Understanding the physical & emotional impacts of stress

Module 2: Designing U

- Self-Care
- Support system
- Balance

This course helps bringing awareness & healthy change to unhealthy and toxic behavioral patterns to enhance the outlook on life and improve overall wellbeing.

Module 3: Building U

- Identify Process to Success
- Toxic Release
- Self-belief/esteem/confidence

This course will teach U how to manage and reduce anxiety mentally, emotionally, and spiritually by building strategies to stabilize emotional wellness

Module 4: Prioritizing U

- Selfishness is OKAY
- Minimizing stress
- Gratitude

This course helps to transition into positive thinking, building resilience, and self-connection.

Module 5: Applying it to U

- Goal setting/Vision
- Planning/ Put it into action
- Target Audience/Niche

This course will bring awareness to the choices and decisions U make that place limits on your success and empower U to change your mind to change your circumstance

Module 6: Improving U

- Transformation
- Transitioning
- Transfer

This course will teach how transforming the mindset will help transition into making better decisions that can transfer into individual success.

Module 7: Completing U

- Execution
- Exercise
- Empower

This course celebrates U. It is about execution, exercising (not physical), and empowering U to use what U learned to UncovertheNewU.

"The Best Investment U Could Ever Make Will Be the Investment in Yourself."

~ Life Coach Nesi

Gem #10:

"The worst thing U can do in life is to give up on yourself."

I wish U nothing but the best and to prosper going forward!

_____
_____
_____
_____
_____
_____
_____
_____
_____
_____
_____
_____
_____

About The Author

SheNesia (Nesi) Ewing is an International Certified Health and Wellness Life Coach, Master Fitness Trainer, and Nutrition Coach. She is a Senior Non-Commissioned Officer (NCO) in the United States Army Reserves. She currently holds a Bachelor of Science in Biology and a Masters in Sports and Health Science with a concentration in sports and exercise performance. She is currently working on her Doctorate in Sports Psychology with an expected graduation date of September 2019.

Along with various degrees, she holds a host of additional certifications to include strength and conditioning, corrective exercise, Zumba, Power Yoga flow, Victim Advocacy, and Master Resilience. Life Coach Nesi is an avid sports fan and exercise fanatic. Life Coach Nesi completed the Dimensioned Wellness Life Coaching School Program in June 2016. And in August of the same year started a sub-entity of her fitness business UncoveringTheNewU; Strength, Health, and Empowerment, LLC also known as S.H.E. As a Life Coach, Nesi desires to teach others how to balance the four components of intentional living and being healthy.

Her goal is to help others make leading a life of optimum health, not a task but simply a LIFESTYLE. She is a Health and Wellness writer in the Life Coach Network Magazine. A contributor to the book "I Want to Quit my Job: 8 Entrepreneurial Tips for Massive Results While Employed,". She has been featured in Dimensioned Wellness Newsletters, Life Coach Network "Coaches Scope," selected as Wellness Life Coach of the Year, Interviewed for Dear Pinq Youtube channel, and Beauty Life and Wellness for Health & Wellness Blogs and fitness tips and multiple podcasts and radio stations. She has been invited to multiple events across Atlanta, GA, Washington DC, Maryland, Virginia, South Carolina, and Texas.

Life Coach Nesi has been motivating and sharing her expertise globally. She has visited Dubai and is preparing for her second International debut in Paris, late 2018. She recently launched her Wellness Improvement Network (WIN) to connect like minds to share tips and tools of how to focus on the individual dimensions of wellness.

www.ingramcontent.com/pod-product-compliance
Lightning Source LLC
Chambersburg PA
CBHW040553010526
44110CB00054B/2671